Ramadaan
and the cheeseboard!

Written by Umm Bilaal Bint Sabir
Content Review @utrujjah_press
Cover Formatting @ilm.cards
Proofreading Umm AbdurRahmaan S. Bint Ahmed and Umm Yunus
Typesetting & Design by Umm Bilaal Bint Sabir

2023 Al Huroof Publishing
© alhuroof
First Published January 2024
2nd Published January 2025
ISBN 978-1-917065-41-2

All enquiries to: alhuroof@hotmail.com
@al.huroof

Al Huroof Publishing

About Al Huroof

Al Huroof is a small project aimed at producing authentic Islamic teaching aids and material. These are based on the Qur'aan and Sunnah, with the understanding of the Prophet Muhammad (sallAllaahu 'alayhi wa sallam), and his righteous companions - Salaf-us-Saalih - (radhiAllaahu 'anhum). After thanking Allaah, Subhaanahu, we would like to thank all those who have aided in this book, from formatting, checking and feedback.

May Allaah accept it as sadaqa jaariyah for us all, ameen.

Dedicated to the childhood antics of three mischievous children!

This book belongs to:

....

It was almost that special time again.

The early mornings. The late nights.

The feeling of hunger and thirst.

The last minute hurriedness

in the kitchen!

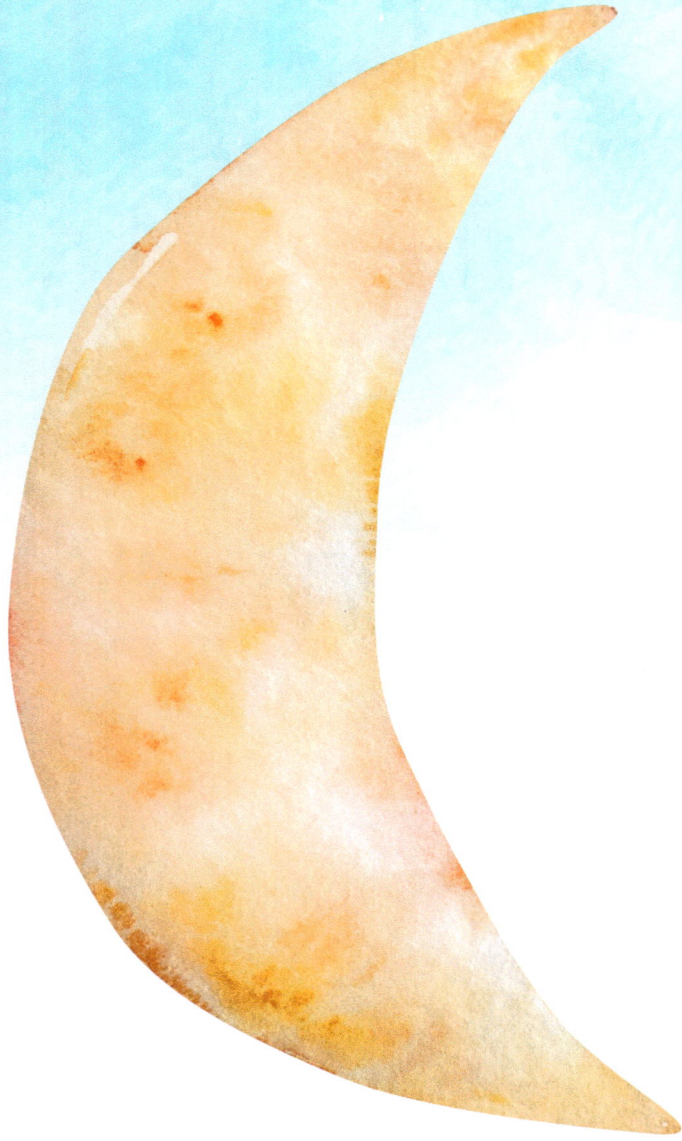

Alhamdullilaah! Yes, it was Ramadaan!

Mum was always telling us about how special this month was even though we never really understood until we were older.

We learned it was the month of

fasting.

"Oh you who have believed, decreed upon you is fasting as it was decreed on those before you so that you may become righteous!"

Surah Baqarah ayah 182

fajr to maghrib

We learned it was the month of
the Qur'aan.

"The month of Ramadaan
in which was revealed the Qur'aan,
a guidance for the people with
clear proofs of (right and
wrong)..."

Surah Baqarah ayah 185

We learned it was the month of
Praying.

It was narrated that Abu Hurairah
(radhi Allaahu'anhu) said:
"The Messenger of Allaah used to encourage
(us) to pray Qiyam during Ramadaan,
and he said:
'Whoever spends the nights of Ramadaan in
prayer (Qiyam) out of faith and in the hope
of reward, he will be forgiven
his previous sins.'"

Sunan an-Nasa'i 2198

We learned it was the month of

du'aa.

"And when My servants ask you ('O Muhammad), concerning Me – indeed I am near.
I respond to the du'aa of the person when he calls upon Me.
So let them respond to Me (by obedience) and believe in Me that they may be (rightly) guided.

It was narrated from Aishah (radhi Allaahu 'anhaa) that she said: "O Messenger of Allah, what do you think I should say in my du'aa on Laylatul-Qadr? He said say:

اَللَّهُمَّ إِنَّكَ عَفُوٌّ

Allaahumma innaka ʿAfuwun

تُحِبُّ العَفْوَ

tuhibbu al ʿAfwa

فَاعْفُوْ عَنِّي

fa'fu ʿanni.

He said say: O Allaah, indeed You are Pardoning, and You love to Pardon so Pardon me."

دُعَاء

It was also special for another reason...

Can you guess why?

Ramadaan was time for the **cheeseboard!**
Not samosas and pakoras – hmm sometimes
kebabs – but a **cheeseboard!**
Some said that wasn't traditional –
but then neither was my mum!
It was her treat.

There were **treats for us too!**
Lots and **lots** of them–**everyday!**

For a whole month!

We were always super excited!

We couldn't wait!

The cheeseboard had Carr's Table Water crackers, ritz, brie cheese and garlic and herb cheese! There was also juicy melon, lychee, mangosteen, some other fruit and hot semolina pudding with cold prunes!

There were pink wafers, jammy dodgers, chocolate biscuits, shortbread, custard creams, chocolate chip cookies …

and Aunty K's carrot cake & spicy fried chicken wings!

Where did mum get all these yummy treats from? Well, it was quite easy!
She just ordered them from the milkman!

milk
cheese
eggs
bread
crackers
biscuits

He would post a leaflet through the letterbox and mum would tick what she wanted and leave it outside the door.

She didn't even have to speak to him – only when it was time to pay the bill!

Everything would be delivered in the
morning – left in a box at the door.
Sometimes we would get there before mum!
We would watch carefully how mum ordered –
it was so easy!

During Ramadaan, there was also another exciting event and that was Ramadaan radio!

My brother took part in a competition and recited
a surah! We muffled our excitement
while he recited! **Yes! He won!**
They never did send the prize though!

That didn't matter! We were so excited
to hear him on the radio, while we were
watching him in the room at the
same time!

even nights

Ramadaan would go by so quickly.

THE LAST TEN NIGHTS

were soon here!

We would be praying to find **Laylat al-Qadr** and hope that our du'aas would be accepted.

We knew this was such a special night, Allaah tells us in Surah Al Qadr (ayah 3)

"Laylat-al Qadr is better than a 1000 months!"

The Prophet (sallAllaahu 'alayhi wa sallam) said: "Whoever spends the night of Laylat al-Qadr in prayer out of faith and seeking reward, all his past sins will be forgiven."

Reference Sahih al-Bukhari 2014 (English) reference: Vol. 3, Book 32, Hadith 231

Something else would also coming to an end

No, not just the **cheeseboard**...

...our
treats
too!

Eid
mubarak

Ramadaan left and we would feel sad but
happy to celebrate Eid!
We celebrated Eid following the Sunnah!

We started with the takbirs the night before –
forgetting them because we were so excited!

The morning would always be a rush – have our
baths, wear new clothes, eat dates and
get to the prayer on time!
Not forgetting the takbirs!

اللَّهُ أَكْبَرُ، اللَّهُ أَكْبَرُ، اللَّهُ أَكْبَرُ
لَا إِلَهَ إِلَّا اللَّهُ
اللَّهُ أَكْبَرُ، اللَّهُ أَكْبَرُ
وللَّهِ الْحَمْدُ

It was narrated from 'Aishah (radhi Allaahu'anhaa) that the Messenger of Allaah (ﷺ) said the Takbir seven and five times in (the prayer for 'Eid) Fitr and Adha."

تَقَبَّلَ اللَّهُ مِنَّا وَمِنكُم

After the prayer we would hug each other out of happiness, but not quite know how to say the du'aa properly! The rest of the day was eating and having fun!

Ramadaan came and left and we would
soon be back to our normal routine.
The cheeseboard was put away and there
would be no more treats for the
next few months –
well that's what mum thought...
until one day!

It was an early Saturday morning when the doorbell rang – it was **the milkman**...

...it was time to pay the monthly bill.

"**£100?!**" mum said in shock.

She was confused! There had been no cheeseboard or treats for a good while – even though she did notice that the bill had been slowly getting **higher** and **higher**!

RECEIPT

£100

TOTAL: ____

"Well," the milkman said, "You ordered: biscuits, a tin of quality streets, cookies, chocolates..." The list went on and on!

You see, it was just so easy! **Wait** for the leaflet, **tick** the things on the list we wanted – **just as mum did** – **wake up** extra early and **collect our treats!**

Before mum woke up!

Did we get into big trouble!

Oh Yes!

Did mum ever forget?

No!

She did find it funny –
a long time afterwards!

Well. that was the end of ordering treats
from the milkman... that all began with
Ramadaan and the cheeseboard!

www.ingramcontent.com/pod-product-compliance
Lightning Source LLC
Chambersburg PA
CBHW041427090426
42741CB00002B/70